I0488842

INTERNATIONAL MILLION$

Winning BIG In The Import Export Business

By: Talia Moore

Library of Congress #

International Standard Book Number:

Talia Moore Enterprise

DT Productions

CONTENTS

INTRODUCTION

I was first introduced to the import/export business back in 2006 when my sisters introduced me to a marketing company called AATCM. AATCM promoted a product called the Turbo Charge; which was a battery operated charger that worked with cell phones to give them an instant charge on the go. The company was interesting and I was into the product, but somehow they could not keep up with the supply and demand of the product which left a lot of distributors who wanted the product out-of-luck. I decided that there had to be a better way to get the product, so I went to the direct distributor and they agreed to sell the product to me at a reduced rate. I was able to get the product and build an army of over 50+ distributors who started coming to me for the hot product.

At one point I got a call from distributors from the Bahamas who wanted a stock of over 2000 pieces. This was by far the most products I had ordered in one shot and we took and filled their order. But, by taking on this order we went one more step further and got in contact with a distributor from China and were able to get the product in our name, which we called "Super Charger" and was able to profit, from getting the supply at a cheaper rate, and created a new relationship with a distributor from china! It was just that simple! I decided that I didn't want to go through a middle man and I went straight to the supplier for the product and the profit from making this strategic move changed the way I thought about purchasing product FOREVER! In this short guide, I will show you how to kickstart your very own import/export business with NO MONEY to start, find a product that sells, and start your business within 24hours! I hope this guide finds you well.

PART 1

FIND A NEED-FILL A NEED

 When I started in the import/export business I found a need in the product of cell phone chargers. In 2006 cell phones were becoming more and more portable and people needed a way to charge their cell phones "on the go." The company AATCM sparked the interest in the product, put it out on the market, had associates to resell the product but, could not keep up with the demand! They could have cornered the market if they had done what I did! Find

a need, and fill it! I realized that people were not giving up on this product (which was in demand), I was interested in the product and I knew in some way that someone had this product in a form that could be purchased at large levels and meet the needs of those who were searching for it But, the question was now where do I get it, what does it cost, and will it make me money in the process? Who was this entity that would meet this demand? The answer was, CHINA! China distributors provided the exact product I needed, at a cost that made me a profit, and satisfied my customers at the same time! If you have a product that you are thinking of that will fill a need in current trends, or a product that will bring a new product to the market; research it, test the market, and if profitable on all sides, GO FOR IT!

PART 2

RESEARCH WORKS

When looking into a product make sure to do your research on the product. This would include the following: trends, styles, reviews and/or feedback, longevity (a short term or long term product), and if the product is in demand. You will find that when you research the product you want to bring to the market, it may have a following already, or you can find a new and improved version of that product that will allow you to create a new way of generating income on that product. In your research you will find that the product you want to bring to the market will essentially work for you (profit wise) and the buyer. If you find that the product is an up and coming product and it would be good to bring to the market then by all means go for it! If you find in your research that the product is on a decline, and there's no viable market for it anymore, LEAVE IT ALONE! If, you don't do your homework on the product that you would like to bring to the market you will find yourself with: debt, product you can't sell, or have product that will cause return and create upset customers. You can research products by searching them in Google, Youtube (video product reviews) Ebay (client feedback) or even other websites that sell the product and what customers are saying about them! If you don't find any results on a product that you want to bring to the market then conduct (if you can afford) a product market survey. This is where you have people test your product for free and get reviews on the product so that when others go to purchase it, they have some prior feedback to reference. So, do your product homework so that you can check your product 100% before placing it on the market.

Here are some websites that you can perform product research on outside of what has been mentioned.

PRODUCT RESEARCH WEBSITES

http://www.consumersearch.com/

http://www.pewinternet.org

http://www.testfreaks.com/

http://www.trustedreviews.com/

http://www.epinions.com/

http://www.consumerreports.org/cro/index.htm

These are a few that will provide with you a quick reference of a product that you have interest in selling and give you a better idea of what the product is worth its weight in import/export gold!

PART 3

IMPORT/EXPORT

Just a few rules about what is the import/export business? When you import goods you are getting goods brought in; or imported from another country. The first things you will have to do are research and identify a product that you like, that product will more than likely come from a manufacture or distributor outside of the United States such as: China, Japan, or India to give you an example. Once you have identified the company/product you want to work with, you purchase the product and then the foreign manufacturer ships the product to you! That's the import business.

In the export business, you create, invent or resell a product to distribute to an overseas buyer. It's that simple! Either way it's a CLEAR TRADE in produce and services from one country to the next. As you read you will understand more about how this process works! Keep reading.

PART 4

MANUFACTURER/ DISTRIBUTOR

 The manufacturer and/or distributor is the product seller. . A manufacture is considered the "main source" of the product. They are the makers of the product, and more than likely will give you the "lowest" cost to purchase because they are the direct source! The manufacture will provide you with not only the product that you are seeking to sale, but with a list of

other products that they manufacture and sell. If you are working with a distributor of the product you wish to sell they may charge a slightly "higher" rate for the product. They are considered the "middle man." They will take longer to ship your product, because they first have to get the product from the manufacture. The manufacture can almost certainly get the product out within days or weeks of you purchasing the product from their company. Sometimes the only way you can tell the difference is by quoting a few suppliers for the product you wish to sell, versus going after the first supplier that sends you a sell sheet.

If you are interested in a product from a chosen manufacture and/or distributor, be sure to ask them for a product sheet as well as a product sample price. The product prices will be slightly higher than the original "bulk" price of the product but, will allow you to test the product before you fully purchasing it.

Even before you attempt to send any money to a manufacturer or distributor, be sure to Google their company, or look at their buyer/seller feedback regarding their products and services. You are purchasing from a foreign country so make sure all of their ducks are in a row!

Here is a list of reputable sources for Import/Export distributors

IMPORT EXPORT DISTRIBUTORS

http://www.made-in-china.com

http://www.alibaba.com/

http://www.dhgate.com

http://www.springimportusa.com/

http://africaimports.com/

http://www.globalsources.com/

These are a few websites that will get you started to find and work with distributors of your choice. These websites works with 1000's of distributors all over the world and provide millions of marketable, upcoming products that you can sell INSTANTLY! It is FREE to connect with these buyers/sellers. Most import directories will ask you to register to connect with them!

The two websites I use the most when picking product and distributors are: made-in-china, and alibaba. You can research and try which ever manufacture you believe is best, but I will still stand by my number one advice: Check them out before you enter a buying relationship!

PART 5

PICKING YOUR PRODUCT

There are a million and one products out on the market that you can choose from! So many trends have made its way to mainstream and have made the trend-hoppers RICH! I'm not saying that you will be rich by picking out the next silicone band, but if you are wise and can read the market trends, you can put out a product that is ahead of its time and ride the cash cow! In my case I picked a product that was hot and on the move! But it's not enough for a product to be hot and up and coming! These are some of the questions you should ask yourself when picking a product: Is the product trending? Will the trend die soon? What will come after it? What's not on the market yet? I was able to read the market with the cell phone product. We knew the single battery charger was not going to make it in the long run! It started to burn out and glitch the phones. The technology was changing, and cell phones were becoming more powerful! Before the battery charger died, we already had the lithium-ion charger ready for sale, which was the next generation of cell phone chargers! We product we bought and sold was called it the Nu-Life Battery Charger. This charger could handle the best cell phones of its day, and lasted LONGER than the single battery charger. This was the future of our product!

Youtube video review of the Nu Life Portable Charger:

https://www.youtube.com/watch?v=0lF0 SHXgvF0

When picking your products make sure your product can last at least 6months-1year if it's a "fad" product. If it's an improvement product make sure it can have a shelf life of 3-5 years or more! This will help you to determine continued success on the product as well as provide you with a goals plan for any changes that may arise during the change or alternate demands of your product.

When ordering your product, as stated before, make sure to "order a sample" and test it to the fullest! Make videos about the results and have other people test the product under many conditions! This will allow you to know if this is the product you want to market and sell!

Be sure to purchase different variations of the product: size, color, orientation, speed etc…provide yourself with a variety so that way you are not stuck with a single product, but a selection of products that you can choose from. Even if you choose to start with one product, be sure to have a list of products from the manufacture that you can sell or provide to customers as an alternate choice. Here is what a product sheet may look like from your manufacture or distributor.

Attribute / Product	Quality	Style	Material	Length/Inch	Color Available	Use	Price/Dollars (FOB)
968/AA	Top	Has Cowlick	100% Human hair (Chinese Hair)	8/16/18	18# / 2#	Hair cut· Hair dyeing· Hair bleaching· Hair perming· Hair drying· Hair straightening· Hair doing up· Bang designing* (Only product with cowlick)· Style designing·	10-30
		No Cowlick		Custom Made	4# /6#		It depends
1702/AA	Top	Has Cowlick	100% Human hair (Chinese Hair)	8/16/18	18# / 2#		10-30
		No Cowlick		Custom Made	4# /6#		It depends
New 1702/AA (Black skin)	Top	Has Cowlick	100% Human hair (Chinese Hair)	8/16/18	18# / 2#		10-30
		No Cowlick		Custom Made	4# /6#		It depends
168/AA	Top	Has Cowlick	100% Human hair (Chinese Hair)	8/16/18	18# / 2#		10-30
		No Cowlick		Custom Made	4# /6#		It depends
New 508/AA	Top	Has Cowlick	100% Human hair (Chinese Hair)	8/16/18	16# / 2#		10-30
		No Cowlick		Custom Made	4# /6#		It depends
Male (With Beard)	Top	Has Cowlick	100% Human hair (Chinese Hair)	8	18# / 2#		15-35
		No Cowlick		Custom Made	4# /6#		It depends
968/A	High	Has Cowlick	100% Human hair & 20% Animal fur	16/18	18# / 2#	Hair cut· Hair dyeing· Hair bleaching· Hair perming· Hair drying· Hair straightening· Hair doing up· Bang designing* (Only product with cowlick)· Style designing·	15-25
		No Cowlick		Custom Made	4# /6#		It depends
168/A	High	Has Cowlick	100% Human hair & 20% Animal fur	16/18	16# / 2#		15-25
		No Cowlick		Custom Made	4# /6#		It depends
508/A	High	Has Cowlick	100% Human hair & 20% Animal fur	16/18	18# / 2#		15-25
		No Cowlick		Custom Made	4# /6#		It depends
New 508/A	High	Has Cowlick	100% Human hair & 20% Animal fur	16/18	16# / 2#		15-25
		No Cowlick		Custom Made	4# /6#		It depends
508/B	High	Has Cowlick	30% Human hair & 30% Animal fur & 40% High Temperature Synthetic Fiber	18	18# / 2#	Hair cut· Hair drying· Hair perming· Hair straightening· Hair doing up· Bang designing* (Only product with cowlick)· Style designing·	10-20
		No Cowlick		Custom Made	4# /6#		It depends
168/B	High	Has Cowlick	30% Human hair & 30% Animal fur & 40% High Temperature Synthetic Fiber	18	18# / 2#		10-20
		No Cowlick		Custom Made	4# /6#		It depends
New 508/C	High	Has Cowlick	30% Animal fur & 70% High Temperature Synthetic Fiber	15/22	18# / 2#	Hair cut· Hair straightening· Hair doing up· Bang designing* (Only product with cowlick)· Style designing·	5-10
		No Cowlick		Custom Made	4# /6#		It depends
968/EC	High	Has Cowlick	100% High Temperature Synthetic Fiber	26	Custom Made (All colors)	Hair cut· Hair straightening· Hair doing up· Bang designing* (Only product with cowlick)· Style designing·	5-7
		No Cowlick		Custom Made			It depends

22

This list will more than likely have the product, the product description, specs, photos of the product and how many pieces they are willing to ship and the price of the LOT. The quantity or LOT is the bulk price of which they are willing to sell the product. Most distributors will generally only allow a few samples, but will be seeking to have you purchase in the product in bulk!

PART 6

PURCHASING

When I started in the import/export business I was lucky enough to have people who wanted my product and so they purchase the product from me upfront!

When purchasing a product you can gain your capital from those who are already interested in the product you have to offer. Collect their funds, buy from the distributor and then when the product arrives ship it to your client! That is a form of using OPM or "Other

People's Money" to start your business. In order to accomplish this form of purchasing you must have a few things in line.

1. An already moving product.
2. A set number of buyers/purchases that will meet your quote demands.
3. A clear established relationship with a foreign manufacturer who's willing to ship in short supply and/or ship direct.
4. An in state (US) distributor who can supply the product at a cost that still allows you to make a profit.
5. Supplier who can ship the product within 5-7days.

If you have at least three out of four of these rules established then using other people's money to secure your product is a "no brainer" to use that method. If you don't have others people's money to secure your product then you should be willing to purchase enough product to promote and sell enough product that will provide instant income that will allow you to purchase more product! When considering your purchase you MUST consider shipping and customs cost or FOB port cost. According to Wikipedia "FOB" means that the seller pays for transportation of the goods to the port of shipment, plus loading costs. The buyer pays cost of marine freight transport, insurance, unloading, and transportation from the arrival port to the final destination."

Usually when you purchase a product the FOB or port cost will be included in the shipping cost. I will discuss more about shipping in the next chapter and how that all works. But, in purchasing your product, know that shipping will be a significant financial factor and must be considered when shipping product through import/export.

Once you have purchased and received your product, test it to make sure it has all its original (intended) functions. Most products from China or other foreign countries will have their native language on the product. If you want your product to appeal to a national audience, be sure to get it personalized so that it reflects a professional English language product. This will be an additional cost, but most manufactures provide custom logos, and print if you purchase product in bulk. Most quantities will vary pending the suppliers minimum purchase amount (s). Be sure to weigh all the cost when considering importing a product. Foreign shipping alone can put you under water if you are not careful!

When purchasing your product from china, their main avenue of receiving funds is through bank wire. This method of funds is used due to the large amounts of money that is (normally) transferred for the product to be shipped. It can also be used for small transactions as well. This is a safe method of transferring funds and is usually transacted through your personal or business bank account. This wire transfer form acts as a "purchase invoice" as well as payment details from their bank to yours! There is a fee that is added from your bank to complete this transaction.

This is an example of a wire transfer form:

e-Weddingbands Wire Transfer Record

Wire Amount (U.S.) $ _____   Date _____ Time _____

#1 - Originator
Name (Customer name)
Acct #
Cash
Address
City State Zip
Tax ID #
ID # & Issuer

#2 – Receiving or Intermediary Bank
Bank Name   (Customer's Bank)
Address
City State Zip
Routing Transit
Swift Code

#3 - Beneficiary	
Name	e-Weddingbands LLC
Acct #	Please call us
Address	3248 N. Canyon Road
City State Zip	Provo, UT 84604

#4 – Beneficiary's Bank	
Bank Name	Zion's Bank
Address	1220 South 800 East
City State Zip	Orem, UT 84097
Routing Transit	124000054
Swift Code	ZFNBUS55

Once you have worked with your distributor the process of wire transfers will become very easy!

Another form of wire transfer could be transacted through Western Union. They do not provide foreign transfers, only domestic transfers from bank to bank. But you can transfer funds personally to your distributor using this method (although not recommended).

The last form of wire transfer could be conducted using an e-payment transfer from companies such as: Paypal, Stormpay, Wepay, or Worldpay. There are many online payment systems, but some foreign distributors may accept them and others may not. But, just keep in mind that the most often used form of payment is a physical bank wire.

PART 7

SHIPPING

As stated before shipping through import/export can be a very "tricky" process. I will walk you through it so that you understand at least the basics of the process. For the most part, like any product you ship you can pre-pay for the shipping with your distributor. They will more than likely add the cost of shipping in their price. This price can be anywhere from $9.00-$1k+ depending on the size and weight of the product that needs to be shipped. China has a few different methods of shipping.

1. Boat (cheap)-But takes 30-40 days

2. Freight (bulk shipping) can take 14-20days. (They will more than likely ship a carton or container full of product using this method)

3. Air (express ship) can take 5-7days and most expensive.

You can have the choice of how you would like to ship your product. The distributors are VERY fair in allowing you to understand how you can ship your product at the lowest cost.

Be aware that if you ship products that contain batteries or that could be hazardous; they will more than likely have to physically go to the nearest shipping port where the package can be searched for safety. If you have a product that will have to be shipped and cannot go "door-to-door" it's best that you find a distributor who has the product in the US or be willing to travel to your local port and wait for your product to clear customs.

As stated before, there are a lot of costs associated with shipping. By forming an import/export business you can sign up for shipping accounts that will allow you to ship your product NOW and pay LATER. Look to these companies for shipping support!

SHIPPING SUPPORT

http://www.ups.com/content/us/en/busso l/browse/ups-small-business/ups-shipping-account.html

http://www.fedex.com/us/oadr/

http://www.dhl-usa.com/en/express/shipping/open_acc ount.html

This are some of the traditional shipping companies you can work to start your import/export business. Some may require general information for you to start shipping with them, and others may require more business related information for verification such as: business license (EIN, DBA, or LLC) Bank account, credit card, or electronic source of payment, working and/or payment relationship with other shipping vendors, and proof of international shipping (payment) relationship.

The best shipping support program to sign up for newbies is UPS! They are simple and do not require that much information to get an account.

If you don't want to create shipping bills, it's best that you purchase your shipping with your distributor. They will always have the BEST rates for you to import your product. If you are exporting your product from the US, the US will have the best rates to ship. It's always the shipping "country of origin" that will give you the best deal.

PART 8

RECEIVING YOUR PRODUCT

 It's always fun to receive your product and know that it has been shipped safe and sound! But, with import/export you may have to go a few steps further to receive your goods.

The first method of receiving your product is "door-to-door." This method is when you receive your product from the foreign distributor, to your front door (home/business) address. In receiving your product in this fashion you skip all

---

the hassle of having to figure out if your product cleared customs or has been sent back for unknown reasons. This is the best form of receiving and will give you INSTANT piece of mind. If you are receiving a product door-to-door you will more than likely pay a premium FOB (port customs cost) before hand and your product, will be a product that can easily be cleared (non-hazardous).

The second method to receiving your product is via freight (carton/container) load and/or hazardous product that must have an in personal customs clearance for it to enter the US port. This method of receiving is not door to door and you must physically go to your local "port customs" in order for the product to be cleared and released to you. There will be paperwork that you must fill out when you arrive, and once the product clears inspection then you are free to take your product.

There is a customs port in almost every major city in the US. Your port will be determined by where you live. The major port freight comes through New York City, NY, and Los Angeles, CA.

You can find out more about international shipping ports at this website: http://www.worldshipping.org/

Once you have received your product, be sure to inspect it for any shipping defects or issues with your product. If you do have shipping issues, be sure to contact your distributor immediately to have replacement defective products.

Once you have established a clear receiving method, ordering and receiving future product will be a cinch!

PART 9

SELLING YOUR PRODUCT

Once you have your product, everything has been inspected and the product is ready to sell, the first thing you must consider is, "Who is your target market?" Is your product something everyone would be interested in like: cell phones, laptops, tablets or other trending electronics? Or does it appeal to kids; like the silly bandz?

      Once you recognize who your target market is, finding a place to sell your product is only a matter of simple research!

When considering selling your products ask yourself these questions:

- Who is my audience (kids, teens, all adults)

- Where are they currently selling your product? (In stores, online, auctions (ebay, craigslist)?

- What season does this product sell the most? (Holidays, Summer, Back To School, Always trending)

- How was your product introduced? (trade show, online review, in-store demo)

- How did people hear about your product? (word of mouth, online ads, in the store, product demo)

- Why would they want to continue buying your product?

Knowing these factors will help you to understand how to sell to your target audience. There a few quick ways to get your product on the market that will help to boost sales. Take these tips in mind.

1. Sell on Ebay (www.ebay.com): Ebay is a quick way of selling your product with vivid pictures, descriptions and even video demos of your product. The avenue provides you an INSTANT AUDIENCE and creates income while you further promote your product. There is a fee after your product has sold.

2. Sell on Craigslist (www.craigslist.org): This is also a quick way to sell your product to a local and international market. This method also provides you instant clients that will be attracted to your product and you can sell as you wish. Free and NO FEE!

3. Sell on Amazon (www.amazon.com) Amazon allows you to sell your product and attach it to a similar selling product for attracting clients.

4. Sell your product as a redistributor on the trader websites (made-in-china, alibaba) to other international distributors. This could bring in bulk sales from other distributors around the world. But, be careful to get permission of the distributor before you resell in bulk on sites where they sell the same or similar products.

5. Sell your product direct to a list of product resellers in the US. This will require research, direct marketing and advertisement to resellers in the US markets.

6. Sell retail of your product in an online store. This will require you to create a website, get hosting, and a POS (point of sale system). The most used FREE POS system is PAYPAL (www.paypal.com).

7. Sell your product in a physical brick and mortal location. This will

require you to rent a space for your: office, product and workers.

When I first started my import business I started it in my living room. I would get shipments and use my dining room table for separation and re-distribution of the product to be mailed to my re-sellers. When my selling operation got too big for my living room then, and only then did I move into an office that would fit the shipments that needed a large area for processing. Where you sell your product is up to you! Be sure to find out the best way to maximize your product, space and overhead! Here are a few low-no cost resources that will help you to get started.

1. Free website: www.weebly.com

2. Domain name: www.godaddy.com (best to get a dot.com)

3. Ebay: www.ebay.com

4. Craigslist: www.craigslist.org

5. Amazon: www.amazon.com

6. Shopify: www.shopify.com

7. Google Merchant Center: https://www.google.com/merchants/signup

These are a few that will get you started in selling your product. The key is to understand how you product is being currently marketed, who is purchasing your product, where are they being purchased, how can I sell in BULK and how long can I continue to sell these products in this manner.

Key: NEVER STOP looking for places to sell your product. The online buyer's stream is practically endless! Find new and innovated ways to get your product to the market, and you will never fall short on your sales goals!

PART 10

MARKETING & ADVERTISMENT

Writing this section will seem like I'm beating a dead horse, because most of the marketing and advertisements I will list have been used over and over. But, they are repeated over and over because they WORK!

When marketing your product you must consider: how the product looks, what are the words and pictures are you using to have your buyer to purchase your product and will it be enough to win their business? The buyer is very VISUAL and will more than likely buy a product from you based off how you market it.

This is an example of a recent product that I marketed and got INSTANT sales results on EBAY. This product netted me over 10k in 5days!

I was able to sell this product so quickly because of the visual appeal of the product! I had clear, up close pictures of the product as well as a full description of the product and what it had to offer the client!

When considering to market your product on eBay or any online website or store, be sure to get PROFESSIONAL PICTURES from your distributor. They will provide you with more than enough visual aids to help you sell the product! They provide you these because they want you also to succeed.

If you are an exporter, then have someone take professional pictures of your product with full details so that the customer will purchase the picture based off what they SEE! This is a poor example of marketing a product.

 This picture is an example of how NOT to market your product. This

picture is dark and dim and does not show the best parts of the bike. You do get an overall view, but a clear view of the bike and its parts will have you sold QUICKER than just seeing it from full shot point-of-view. When marketing and advertising your product, make sure you have complete and CLEAR facts about the product and product description. Include all the details your client/customer would like to know about your product as well as a full sell sheet that provides pricing and a contact: name, phone, e-mail, and fax number to close the sale.

In the same way your physical advertisement should reflect a clear product that is attractive and one that your customer is ready and willing to buy. Here are a few places you can advertise your product. The

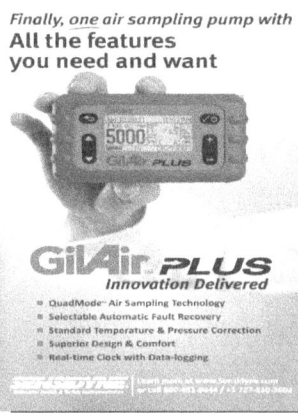

average marketing can make your product move in 2-3weeks. The EXCEPTIONAL marketing can make your product move in DAYS!

Here are a few ways to market your product:

- Facebook
- Twitter
- Instagram
- LinkedIn
- Pinterest
- Google Plus (G+)
- Blogging
- Forums
- Youtube (do a product review)
- Vine (micro-video)
- Build An App
- Direct Marketing
- E-Mail List Serve
- Phone Call (cold calls)

There are a MILLION ways to market your product. The only limitation is what work you are willing to put in to get your product to the market.

Sample Video Product Review:

 A product review provides a clear visual of the product, how the product can be used as well as the full detailed use of the product. Google some sample product reviews to get an idea of how one looks. Once you have selected your product, set up a video demo so that other can also see how your product works, and you will be rewarded with SALES!

PART 11

INTERNATIONAL MILLION$

So many people ask me about how I made money in this business, the truth is I have failed in this business, and I have been VERY successful at this business. With anything you do it's all about constancy, and keeping yourself a head of the curb!

There are millions of products that people are ready to purchase from you, the REAL question is, are you ready to bring it to the market?

Find out what product you LOVE, research it, find the proper distributor and go from there! If you are a trend hopper, look to find new products that have not hit the market yet that you can capitalize on them! There are so many foreign products that have yet to hit the US soil.

If you are going to get into this business it's best to find a niche. By finding a niche product, you will more than likely stay consistent in that market and have people purchasing from YOU over and over. If you choose to have an online store, or sell more than one product, be sure you can handle the demand of all your products and keep inventory as needed. It's best to stick with an ale carte product line and keep the "most popular" in stock and order as needed for the remainder of your product.

Can you start this business overnight and start making THOUSANDS and the answer is YES! I'm a witness that it can happen!

With import, it's all about the product relationships. Make sure you are in constant connection with your distributor. A good distributor will be willing to answer all your questions and get back to your promptly. Be sure to respond to them just as quickly and your import relationships will remain strong.

Find a product you can manage. If the product is too much for you to handle, you will soon find yourself backing away from the business and become disgruntled by the process.

Start SMALL! If you don't have deal with overhead, DON'T! If you don't have to hire employees, DON'T! Minimize all your cost, so all you see is profit. Work with OTHER PEOPLES MONEY to purchase the product as well as create a revenue stream for your business.

Use ALL forms of FREE social media outlets to promote and sell your product. This will provide an audience that will be attracted to your product, review your product and encourage others to do the same. Maintain your social connections and reward them for their loyalty to your product as often as you can afford.

Here are 30 steps, tricks and advice you can use today to become an INTERNATIONAL IMPORT/EXPORT MILLIONARE tomorrow!

- Find a product you love, that is trending or is an easy sale.

- Locate a distributor that will be willing to produce the product and ship within five-seven days or less at minimum cost.

- Order a sample and create video demos test on the product.

- Create marketing for the product.

- Create a website that promotes your product.

- Find 20 resellers who would be willing to sell your product and purchase (in advance) at a bulk rate.

- Market your product on the open social market.

- Get your product and quickly redistribute to your resellers.

- Get product feedback and have them recorded to your social media and website to create more buzz!

- Develop multiple streams to sell your product online for residual income.

- Take your produce to the open market and test it! (trade show, mall, open market)

- Video record your results, response and feedback.

- Create a full resellers/affiliate program based on the purchasing trends (selling results).

- Allow the product to take flight by allowing others to sell your product as you continue to research more products that will compliment your hot selling item!

- Continue this cycle until you are completely successful from this product and have sold so many you have hit millionaire status!

- Stay consistent and do not go back and forward from product to product.

- Communicate with your buyers and sellers and give 100% customer service on your product.

- Speak often and positive about your product to others. This energy alone will propel your product and selling power!

- Build trust with your foreign distributor so that your purchasing transactions will run smoothly.

- Have an open return policy that allows the customer to have a fair advantage if there is an issue with your product.

- Be sure to replace, fix or provide a full refund of the product is not 100%.

- Be generous! Out of the millions you make, be sure to give.

- Provide incentives to your resellers, customers and other frequent buyers.

- Manage your money WELL or it will overtake you! Create an accounting system that works for you so that you understand your net and gross profits!

- Be care about your product and NEVER go off your word in building your business.

- Success is only a bi-product of the work that goes into a venture.

- You need the help of others to grow your business! You can NOT do it alone.

- Always be respectful, they don't have to accept or purchase from you or with you.

- Keep a leveled head. Money is NOTHING…relationships are everything. Keep them first and you will always be a success!

- Be the FIRST! When finding or bring a product to the market be the first to introduce it to the market. This provides leverage and sustainability.

- Don't give up! It's not a tough game to get into, but it can beat you up if you get in over your head. Find out what works for you, then go with it!

PART 12

CONCLUSION

In conclusion, I have enjoyed the success I learned from being in the import export business. I was not taught this in school, or a business course! I was taught by trial and error.

I hope this quick-guide provided you with the tips needed to get you started in the import export business and the know how to do it TODAY!

I always hated going online and trying to find information about a topic I was interested in that read books 10x as long as this book and provided me with NO forward moving information.

I hope this guide finds you well and that you are able to profit, and have it bring fruit into your life! It's such a joy to be in business for yourself. The freedom of know that you help bring something that someone loved to the market, or that you have the ability to make a living at it!

With over 8years in the import export business I'm thrilled to share this information and knowledge with you! Please be sure to share this information with someone else who maybe considering working online or selling productions through import export trading.

Thank you and God Bless You.

Jeremiah 29:11- "For I know the plans I have for you," declares the Lord, "plans to prosper you and not to harm you, plans to give you hope and a future."

Appendix

Wikipedia Online-Definition of POS

Photos Pulled from Google Images.

Scripture From Biblegateway.com NKJV